STATIONS ALONG MY
TRAIN
OF THOUGHT

A Collection of Poetry by

PARKER J TILLMAN

DEDICATION

To my father, Roosevelt Tillman.

You were many things to me—too many to list here. I don't know if this book would have been the same without your influence. Through life's capsizing tides, you helped me tread dark waters, and I know you were proud to do it. Though I second-guess myself, I take comfort in knowing you always had faith in me. Now, I must have that faith in myself.

You are forever in my thoughts and will always dwell in my heart.

I love you so much, Dad.

ACKNOWLEDGMENTS

Creating *Stations Along My Train of Thought* has been an intensely personal journey, one I could not have undertaken alone.

To my family—thank you for being my foundation. Your support and encouragement kept me steady through every page. To my late father, Roosevelt Tillman, whose love and pride continue to guide me—this book is as much a tribute to you as it is a reflection of my journey.

To my friends who believed in this project from the start, thank you for your unwavering faith and for being the first to share in my words. To everyone who helped refine this book, thank you for your thoughtful insights, patience, and dedication to helping me bring this work to life.

And to every reader who boards this *Train of Thought*—thank you. I hope these words offer you a moment of connection, comfort, or inspiration along the way.

PREFACE

Stations Along My Train of Thought is a collection born from some of the most turbulent times in my life. For years, I smothered my emotions until they became toxic, relying on distractions and poor coping mechanisms to keep the feelings at bay. It was a cycle that kept me from facing what I truly needed.

During those times, writing became my sacred refuge—the one place where I could find clarity. Each word I wrote allowed me to release what I couldn't say out loud. Though I still carry fear and uncertainty, allowing these words to exist and writing without restraint became a powerful form of healing.

Whatever you need to open your heart and find peace, I pray you discover it too. In these pages, I hope you'll find moments that resonate and remind you of the beauty in expressing what's within. The world is a better place with you in it.

Now Boarding: The Train of Thought

CONTENTS

HAIKUS

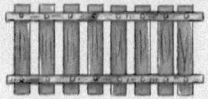

Japanese poems of seventeen syllables

"Expression doesn't always need to be long form. When I wrote these haikus, it felt like I was engaging in a puzzle—trying to maximize each word, each syllable."

TOMORROW MAYBE

Present's gift is tossed
away by expectance of
tomorrow's present.

OUT OF HABIT

I think about you;
my version of you, rather
just out of habit.

FRAGILE

I truly wonder
how many times I will crack
before I shatter.

LIPS

Tender kisses for
the soul never seems to go
away or astray.

PAIN

Pain pain go away
don't come back another day
please just stay away.

BABY FACE

Such young innocence
can only be reflected
by their purity

HELP YOU FALL

In life, you've fallen
it is time to fall again,
try to fall for me.

SKIN CONDITION

My skin fits me well
but, within my skin, I feel
uncomfortable.

STATION I

Poems of Life Experiences, Perspective, Low Self-Esteem, Self-Discovery, Self-Empowerment, and Isolation

"I have been both the meek and the proud. It wasn't life that dictated that—I know it was by my design. We are the conductors."

ENOUGH

Am I strong enough?
Am I wise, patient, or kind?
I really hope so.

DOUBLE EDGED

It's wielded as a sword, under my ward.
Its power is a mystery, a mettle forged by history.

Fiery cannot describe my weapon's temper.
Forged in light and darkness the imperfections
still linger.

My weapon can both create and destroy,
This weapon wielded by a lost black boy.

Quenched by tears of joy and struck by frustrated
screams, my weapon battle-tested in extremes.

Every moment and every beat, its power unfolds,
The memories, reflections, and stories it holds.

Its temperament etched in gleaming steel,
Reflecting both the joys and the pains of ordeal.

Regrets, tragedies, a surface scarred by years,
Stains of the past, sheathed in fears.

It cannot be dismantled, nor torn apart,
my double-edged heart, a work of art.

SKIN

I spend way too much time uncomfortable in my
own skin, knowing within,

I am truly extraordinary, so why do I act ordinary?

With my abilities questioned, my potential
confined, The capabilities of my creative mind.

Human nature, a relentless and critical part,
Is never satisfied at the very start.

When did my self-esteem become so weak?
Who else would find more quirks so unique?

I need to embrace where I have not been,
Cherish my quirks, my flaws, and my skin.

It may at times feel tight,
But I must embrace my skin, my being, my right.

THE CLASSROOM

The professor continues his lecture,
There are no words, works of art, or architecture.

As captivating as you.

You sit beside me, and I cannot help but wonder,
How to get your number.

Should I drop my pen just within your reach?
That cliché is hard to beat.

I should ask your opinion on the last thing spoken!
Since the ice between us remains unbroken.

In your eyes, lies a soul, I long to explore,
The person you are, who I have come to adore.

Lost in thought, the end of class was found.
The knowledge I lacked, yet my adoration was
profound.

I SEE YOU

I see you as we walk the same hall,
But as I grow near, your eyes fall from the floor to
the wall.

You didn't have to try so hard to avoid my gaze,
And yet, I considered that it was just a phase.

Yet, as soon as I passed you by,
To the next person you cross,

You said, "Hi."

I don't know if you knew,
but I could see you.

BROKEN

Sorrowful mourning, of such a lovely life, I
endured all kinds of strife.

I was polite, well, in the confines of socialites.

In my mind, I was a bit grim,
Constantly floating in murky waters,
unsafe to swim.

Trapped and broken, I wished to live again.

Find me in the shadowy depths,
bring me to the light.
I'm tired of my consistent sleepless night,

Rolling around in the midnight moonlight,
To the unwelcome sting of sunlight.
Solitude is only a symptom of this pit, why does
brokenness fit?

The puzzle that lacks a piece?
There is no peace for pieces that cannot form a
masterpiece.
I want to be awoken, but first.
I must fix whatever inside may be broken.

A TRICK TODAY

I learned a new trick today; I created a mask to keep my feelings away.

The Mask treads a path where emotions dare not follow, chains bind my heart, a catacomb so hollow.

The Mask holds the art of stoic grace, a facade so perfect, it hides my true face.

My Mask, a canvas, emotionless, serene, no cracks, no creases, no emotions in between.

My Mask showed me how to walk away, from the color of love's sweet warmth to the shadows' gray.

I dance along mournfully to my fateful beat;
silence has guided my two left feet.

I control my breathing, silence my cries,
bury my truth beneath My Mask of lies.

I've bottled my feelings, sealed them tight,
locked away, hidden from the world's sight.

The echoes of laughter, the tears I used to cry,
now sealed in glass jars, where emotions lie.

The Mask has become beyond my control, the
strength I thought I'd found bore a hole in my soul.

AWARENESS

Self-reflection is a key part of awareness.

I am aware that I am taller than the average,
I am aware that in my life I have incurred a lot of
damage,

Whether it be internal or external,
Physical or emotional,

I am aware of all the scars,
I am aware that when I'm hurting, I look for the
stars,

Because I wish to be anywhere that pain will not
follow,
Pain that roots deep into my soul leaving it
hollow,

I am aware that on the outside I can intimidate,
For that reason, I am reluctant to initiate,

Any form of contact...first,
My scars are reminders of all the worst,
Mistakes that I have made and had to learn from,
I am aware that the effects of these mishaps
make me numb,

And because of this, I struggle to engage,
And socialize properly with others my age,

Aware of life's battles, both outer and within,
Aware they etched their tales into my soul, my
skin.

LOOK AT ME

You can see me, I'm hard to miss, but you let me be,
Fear of what you see prevents any kind of chemistry,

I guess it doesn't matter; it's not like science is
your major.

Look at me and read my story page for page,
I promise you won't get bored, even at my
young age.

You'll be surprised when you see what I've been
through,
And when you are through, you will see your
opinions were untrue.

I do not give the opportunity to all,
And some pages have been torn out because of
how low I can fall.

Some reject my cover, at times, it is hard to recover,
So, I close my book, so they can no longer,

Look at me.

FLEETING PERSPECTIVE

I was always aware of how I was perceived,
How could it be, that after all this, I never believed?

That I could change that view,
and be the man that I wanted to be.

I'm not a beaver; I couldn't give a damn,

Where you stand,
and where your perception will land.

All I know is that from this day on,
I'm going to be moving on.

So, wherever you stand to judge me,
I have moved beyond what you could initially see.

A LIFE WORTH LIVING

I reside in my fantasies, not your fallacies.

I live my life in its entirety, because inside of me
lies possibilities.

Possibilities to possibly find me, but probably.
Finally, find the key, to this cage that
smothers me,

It inhibits me from potentially unlocking the
potential that lies in me.

Protect me from your protection, I don't want
your lesson.

Discussing who I am to be, I live for me.

I look at you and you look back; I see that all you
see is black.

It's written all over your facial expression,
That you wished I was locked away in government
detention.

I refuse to be that guy; I refuse to live that lie.

I promised my mama, I wouldn't be,
anything less than exemplary.

If I listened to you, and you told me,
exactly who I was supposed to be,

Who is living my life?
Because it damn sure wouldn't be me.

COLORS

They say, "You talk white."
Why is that the only color that represents my
intellect and insight?

My skin they see as black, but can't they see?
It's just a hue, not the entirety of me.

Brown, my skin, a canvas of years,
melanin-filled joy, layered with fears.

Social stigma and stereotypes keep us apart, yet
diversity and friendships are crafted works of art.

My gender is a shade of blue,
beyond my shade, I hold a spectrum too.

I blend and adapt in nonfiction,
to weave a world of hues and diverse diction.

The color of my words and how they shed light,
the inclusion of content, depth, and insight.

For within me, dwells a world, unseen, colors of
thought, emotion, reserve, and obscene.

GOD, the creator, knows my soul's true hue,
blanketed in love, compassion, and virtue.
Our colors of light and dark, in every hue,

What colors deep down reside in you?

CULTURE

My parents sent me to school to learn who I
could be,
but some of these white folks couldn't
possibly see.
I'm black and proud to have melanin flowin'
in me.

Now I'm searching for a lost culture,
Discover my past for my future.

With Malcolm X, empowerment echoes from the
past,
With Martin Luther King, I believe, my dream will
last.

Educated by the hands that hold the strings,
Yet I refuse to let their influence cling.

To follow their laws, flawed, and skewed,
In a land, where black lives are misconstrued.

I can't live their white lives or bear their white lies.

Luck has it that this ain't where the line will end,
I'm tired of living in the land of pretend.

I won't let the narrative be spun,
Won't yield to the lies, won't come undone
Shit is wrong, the news sings the same song.
How black people are dying, and the police are
trying.

My father taught me to tread paths as a black
man with reach,
By doing what "majority white," teachers couldn't
teach.

He taught me to stand tall and work hard for my family,
My dad was a visionary, the apple didn't fall far from the tree.

A shock to the society I aim to be.
A strong, successful black man, tenacious and free.

I'd rather stand out, than be a regular nigga, looking for a handout.

SPEECHLESS

At least today, I cannot convey,
The words trapped in my mind and heart.
But from the start, I found my voice in one
particular art.

With poetry, I can finally impart
What I think and feel without falling apart.
I hope my words play their part,

To show you what I cannot.
This is my one-shot

To reveal who I am inside,
To show how your struggles and mine coincide.

But that's not why I write about my side.
If I hadn't found this outlet, I might not have
survived.

So, I thank GOD I finally realized,
That my voice could be materialized.

STATION 2

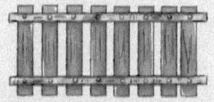

Poems of Dating & Love –
The Highs & Lows.

The Triumphs & Mistakes

"I have loved, and I have lost. Sadly,
I continue to carry some of those
memories as scars. I treat them like
warning signs, but they shouldn't be.
Trends may feel the same sometimes,
but that's why we have faith."

STUPID LOVE

If I could get back
time I spent thinking of you.
I would think of you.

DOMINOES

I learned to fall as I learned to stand,
Back in adolescence, with a supporting hand.

In kindergarten, I learned unrequited love
Her presence consumed me, all I desired to
think of..

Showing genuine kindness and care,
Hoping she'd realize **I** was there.

As I grew older falling hurt more,
The bigger the heart, the harder the floor.

Scrapes, Scars, and bruises, my gifts from the land,
With trembling resolve, I sought the will to stand.

If falling is what I was born to do,
I'll rise and stand upright again, for when I fall
for you.

FIRST POEM

Standing here,
All I could think,
Is of my heart that goes boom,
Every time we meet,
The smile that grows across my face,
As I look in your dark brown eyes,
Even though these feelings are new,
I just want you to know,
I care about you.

DATING

Dating, a mix of fate and heart,
an urge and whim, we naturally start.

Emotionally, it's a swirling sea, turbulent waters
wild and free.

Habitually, it's on borrowed time, success or
failure, a ticking clock, to foster love by the
destined chime.

Financially, it costs to please, among fine dining,
luxurious dates, and gifts, for social ease.

Mentally, it sucks... it's a puzzle, a paradigm, a
paradox.

Physically, I hold my ground,
yet within my emotions, I am unbound.

But then again, If I were to fall again,
my dating trend would finally end.

TINDER

Swipe right,
I should swipe...right?
Swipe left,
If I swipe...what's left?
Oh, you're cute!
Oh, I accidentally swiped left...shoot.

I know if I like you within five seconds, with no
cause to be hesitant.
Although I know, it's unfair to make such an
assessment in an instant.

If I am on the fence, I will check your personality,
How is it possible for 500 words to be enough to
know your reality?

I swipe, you swipe,
And we may or may not match.
That would be the catch.

That if I swipe left and you swipe right,
We'll never connect, and in hindsight.

I might've loved to know you,
Maybe I would've loved to love you too.

So to all those who wanted to get to know me.
I am truly, sorry,

True connections can be hindered,
When swiping on Tinder.

LIFE

To create generations, with a sweet foundation,
love is discovered, or at least a lustful exploration.

Man and woman discover fascination.
He offers his transportation, to her destination,
She welcomes him with anticipation,
A biblical union profound, for a divine creation.

They nurture life, a shared obligation.
A birth of heart without hesitation,
In passion's hearth, they found their salvation.

It's a tale as old as time, a sweet narration.
A tale in my poetic translation.

I TRIPPED...

When I tripped
It was inevitable that I'd fall in love with you.

It wasn't the moment that you stated that you
"loved me,"

I'm not so narcissistic that your confession would
coerce my heart to fall into your lap.

It was already yours, built upon a foundation of
your presence cemented into my core.

The sound of your voice echoed throughout the
caverns of my soul,
And the words you said way before "I love you,"
that had already paid my lover's toll.

It was your smile that could shed a light into all
places I would attempt to recede within myself,
A smile so bright you'd find me immediately
hiding in plain sight like a book on a shelf.

When I fell for you, my heart had already stated
"I love you too."

Every time I looked into your eyes and found
something new that I loved,
That simply reinforced the fact I had found my
beloved.

The next time I discovered my love for you,
I was embraced by the pleasant warmth of your hands,
Falling for you was never in my plans.

But when I tripped for you,
I fell into a state of happiness I didn't know I
could access, but it's true.

Before
    I
        fell....
            you
                tripped
                    me...

FEAR

When you came into my life,
You brought my two greatest fears.
Joy and Hope had filled me with strife,
For after they had gone, the only feeling I had was
the moist sensation of my tears.

This sounds very dramatic I know,
but have you ever fallen in love like the snow?

Fallen so gracefully and delicately it seemed
impossible to break?

I hope not, but it seems we are too alike for that.

You came at a time when clouds were dark,
When my skin was as thick as bark.

When the music had a little less beat,
when sugar was a little less sweet.

And I felt that I would not need anyone,
because anyone would not need I,

I still hope you complete me.

I don't know how long you'll be mine,
But for now, in your love, I feel divine.

NOT LOVE

"I love you," is what I'd like to say.
It's too easy, its simplicity vexes me!

How about..."We."
Open to many interpretations in various situations.
It's scary, what I feel for you may be temporary.
We are together, yet probably not forever...

I don't know what your love is,
I don't expect to understand, like a question on a
pop quiz.

But I want to, I want you.
And from what I know of love, what we have is a
similar feeling of.

With you, I'm vulnerable; my heart thinks you're
adorable.
And it is just as exciting as it is terrifying,
But it would be ratifying.

If I learned how to love like you do.
To be someone for you.

I don't know the proper way to show how far my
adoration for you goes by the miles,
I will keep track with your smiles.

"We," will last as long as the adventures and
stories we'll tell,
I'm past fell.

How about I tell you what I love?
Your hair that smells of adventure in the deep
forest next to a campfire,
Your voice filled with energy as if it could never
tire.
You are full of life; I love that I want to live to love
our adventures.

"We," is a word that holds a collection of grand
treasures.
Let me show you what "We," can do:
"We can sing,"
"We can dance,"
"We can romance,"
"We can love."
"We are great together," they bet.
So instead of saying, "I love you,"

Which is true,
I believe "We," have so much to look forward to.

ROSE

You're more than just a pretty sight,
A rose, adorned in thorns, dark and bright.

I tread with care, your essence, I adore,
A beauty unique, a metaphor.

In your petals, a universe lies,
In the depths of your soul, where darkness resides.

You may appear, just like the rest,
Yet your thorns hold a secret zest.

A silent power, a warning there,
In your gaze, a world so rare.

Your thorns, I respect, each sharp sting,
A reminder of the pain your love can bring.

I won't mistreat you, I understand,
The scars you bear, the trials firsthand.

Others tried and failed, I know,
The wrath of the rose, its endless woe.

But I'll embrace you, thorns and all,
In love's sweet rise and bitter fall.

Bleed me, I offer, my heart at your feet,
Hour after hour, our love, will be sweet.

I'll carry you and your thorns, as long as it will
take, I know what it's like to have a petal break.

I promise, not to drop you, if your darkness
doesn't get brighter,
If your thorns begin to dig into my skin, I'll just
hold tighter.

Take your time, my Rose, to choose,
In love, there's nothing we can lose.

My heart, my soul, to you I propose,
To you, my dearest, beautiful Rose.

TENSION

I can feel you
The way your fingers graze my skin, a touch akin,
To longing deep, where your hunt begins.

I can see you
Your eyes darting, from mine to my lips,
A predator poised, with sultry hips.
Each breath I take is stolen in sips.

I can hear you
Your heartbeat is quick, unrelenting,
And your voice is trembling, confiding, softening,
To a whisper, each word unraveling, dissolving,
Until silence stalks, its tension cementing.

I move closer,
I've never felt both safe and in danger before,
Your words are gone, but your presence I can't
ignore.
Your longing was mine, felt in every pore.
I can not take the tension anymore,

As your hand rises, slow, deliberate,
To rest on my cheek, our moment intimate.

I close my eyes,
And I realize

You finally caught me.

OUR SPACE

Your body neatly tucked in my arms,
The blissful silence, full of its many charms.

I feel complete, where time is no longer
important,
At this moment,

I could freeze time and be forever satisfied,
With the feeling of your warm body pressed
against mine,

As you lie in my arms against my chest,
Your shallow breaths feel like whispers to my
heart,

I will have lived a life both whole and happy,
I don't ever want to leave,

And even when we do have to leave this comfort,
I take comfort in the presence of this memory.

WHAT IS LOVE?

I tried to grasp love,
It's elusive like fluttering butterflies or a restless
dove,

It can be Attraction,
Affection, Passion, yet that definition,
Doesn't sit well with me,
Because what I see, when you smile,
It makes life worthwhile.

I lived my life to meet and love you,
And eventually, I hope you feel the same way too.
You're more than a feeling, a hope, or a thought,
In your love, my fears are all for naught.

In you, I've witnessed love's face,
Defined not by words, but by your embrace.

Love is your laughter, your touch, your sigh,
Love is together, through our valley low, and our
mountainous high.

So, in your arms, I know what love is,
Love is you.

MISGUIDED

I thought I knew you, that I held the key,
To fully comprehend your complexity.

Instead of embarking on understanding,
I was lost in your labyrinth, left simply standing.

There were times when I did get it right,
When we talked throughout the night.

But I faltered, misunderstood your silent plea,
I failed to grasp what you truly needed from me.

You didn't want me to spend a dime,
All you needed was quality time.

How selfish of me to think,
That physical pleasure would strengthen our link,

Our bodies entwined,
Yet, I missed the depths of your heart and mind.

I didn't spend enough time holding you in my
arms,

It's belated, but I apologize for the wounds I've
caused,
For the moments I didn't reside in, the time I did
not pause.

My ignorance brought harm to my love, and I now
realize, the pain that lies within your silent cries.

I'm sorry for being oblivious, my guilt will not
rest,
I provided love, but time I failed to invest.

In my heart, the regret weighs like a heavy load,
For the love I gave, but the time I never bestowed.

STATION 3

*Poems of Heartbreak, Resentment,
Frustration, Insecurity, and Distrust*

*"There isn't any sugarcoating this.
It is a horrible feeling, but we all
get here eventually. These are my
scars, but they were necessary for
my growth. I know that now."*

MISSED CALLS

You haunt my cell phone.
Your random calls and brief texts,
break my soul each ring.

ERASER

I'd love to wipe the slate clean
Memories,
Both our successes and tragedies,
Etched across my mind.

I place my hand over my head,
As if my touch alone could erase what lingers there.
But no—
It simply smears.

The fears,
Of being captive to this board,
Make me...
That's just it—
I don't have the words.

I remove my hand and see the smudges,
Brought to life by my tears.
And as I sob,
As I close my eyes tightly, trying to turn away,
As I search in vain for that magic eraser,
The weight on my chest reminds me:
I cannot erase her.

WHEN I LOST YOU (KISS)

When I lost you,
Our last kiss left a taste of pity on my lips.
It tasted of tears that were shed and tears that
soon would be.

When I lost you,
You seemed to look right through me with eyes
that cried goodbye...like I had already gone.

When I lost you,
You knew that we would never be the same. You
cried for the past that hoped we had a future.

When I lost you,
I found it no gift being in the present. And
presently, the storm outside would not even begin
to compare to the storm raging within.

When I lost you,
Words were nothing more than wasted breath. If
only I knew the day you took my breath away at
the beginning of the end, maybe I could have held
my breath a little better.

When I lost you,
I became bitter. Because, unlike you, I did not
have a backup lover to lick my wounds.
I had only the tears that seeped their way into
my cuts which pained me until the screaming
became inaudible.

When I lost you,
I lost you for good and not a single new miss,
Could remove the taste of pity from our last kiss.

WEIGHT

When we began,
I could lift the weight of our love with one tightly
cupped hand,

When we parted,
The hand that held on so firmly, grew weary.

When you came back,
Our weight, like sand, slowly slipped through my
fingers.

I scooped you into my two tightly cupped hands
And tried again to hold on to us.

PERFECT STRANGER

Time doesn't heal wounds completely,
Scars leave constant reminders of our memory.

Our chapter has ended, yet the torn pages flutter,
Casual comments tend to trigger.

Ours was an end in the time period,
periodically people place prime positions on my
predicament.
And honestly, tend to piss me off or at least, fill
me with resentment.

How can they grasp the depth of our shared years?
Burned bridges bring lasting destruction,
Relationships crumble with no hope of
reconstruction.

Your voice, once the melody in my heart,
Now just a reminder of what tore me apart.

Your touch, once engraved on my skin,
Will fade too, like a cheap tattoo.

From late-night tussles under warm sheets,
To cold nods and awkward greetings on the
streets.

Your eyes, which once held love so strong,
Now avoid mine, where did we go wrong?

Our hearts unraveled; Our love waivered.
You were my perfect lover, now you are a perfect
stranger.

PIECES

Go ahead, shatter my heart! Let it fall, tear it apart.
See it break on the cold, hard floor in pieces, it
cries, in pain, it implores.

"It hurts!" it screams loud and clear,
"Help me!" it pleads for someone near.

Its cries echo, filling the room, a symphony of
heartbreak in the gloom.

I hush my heart, its cries I muffle, yet its pain
refuses to stifle.

But it's alright, you never knew,
Our love, our bond, is forever true.

You failed to grasp our symphony's song,
Yet in my heart, you still belong.

Now it's just me and him, my broken part,
Embracing every shattered shard.

"Fear not," I whispered, cradling his woes,
"She's gone, but our love eternally flows."
With tender hands, I gather each piece,
In love's mending, our pain finds release.

"We'll rebuild every fragment and part,
For our love, my dear heart is a work of art."
In pieces or whole, love never ceases,
Even in fragments, its strength increases.

EMPTY

My soul is destitute, there is little I can do to
contribute,

To fill the space that drives me mad,
rather than be sad,

I will find new outlets to relieve the stress,
So, I no longer suppress.

The words that my heart screams,
That my mind replays in my dreams,

I must be the one to see my soul half full,
So, when love comes it is a natural pull.

Rather than forced or the product of coerce,

When I fall in love again, that love will contend,

With the love I have for myself in plenty, full or
empty.

LOST LOVE

I bury myself in my bed and ponder what you said,
I wonder what happiness lies ahead, hoping
beyond hope that my happiness isn't dead,

All the signs you gave me that went unread,
I could finally comprehend what you said,

Coming to that realization, I should have fled, but
my limbs were as heavy as lead,

But you don't understand what's going on in my
head, the solitude I truly dread,

You were never on the same side of my bed, the
cold between us began to spread,

The distance between us is now so far apart, even though we were so close at the start,
The thought of losing you aches my heart, the love we once had was a work of art,

It is now time for us to depart, keeping my distance may be smart,
So, I can rebuild my walls that fell apart, a small piece of my heart to you I impart,

So, as I lay alone in my solitude crafted throne,
I am left to recuperate on my own, the pain you caused cannot be atoned,

I don't know why but even if my life gets back on track, I'd take you back,

Lost within, with no map to guide my way, in this labyrinth of self, I find my stay.

WORDS

Words have power,
Yet I cannot find a single,
Word in my arsenal,
To make you stay,
WHAT CAN I SAY?

Please?
Cease!

I need you with me, I still love you, baby,
Pathetic is the word to describe how I felt,
But that doesn't matter,
Because my heart was the orator,

Can you hear it?
Hear it cry, its mournful song, as half of me is
cruelly gone.
Can you see it?
Desperately grasping for its other half,
At this moment nothing else matters more than
staying whole,
Fulfilling the soul,

Yet you tore away,
And my heart grew quiet,
It became speechless,

Now whatever words are used,
To try and restore its voice,
Are spoken to deafened ears.

SORRY FOR THE TRUTH

She doesn't need me anymore,
I am not even certain, feigned ignorance can
ignore.

I still need her, the warm memories only linger,

And as my cold heart warms, it continues to
crack, Longing for her love to come back.

The resentful wall is much too tall, I can't grasp
the meaning of it all,

Hope is my burden through this endeavor,
But I cannot accept the hope any longer,

You moved on and continue to try to be happy in
the midst of another guy.
So why can't I?

Why am I bound to you so tightly? Bound to think
about you daily and nightly,

I don't want us to completely unravel,
I'm stuck at a crossroads with no idea where to
travel.

I miss you dearly, and I see so clearly,
How important that you are,
as I have contemplated this far,

I just want you to know that I ...
I'm sorry for the truth.

ELEVEN

One is the loneliest number,
Especially after another one has done a number
on it and decides to separate,
Size no longer appropriate,

They were once eleven,
And now one stands oddly alone next to an even,
One has met a variety of other numbers,

Twos through nines just didn't seem to measure,
One felt no stronger expression,
Then the happiness one felt as part of eleven.

WANT YOU

Whatever heart I have left to spare, I hold it close
and would not dare,

To give up the last remaining piece, I fear the
inability to find peace.

The chunk sizes seem to increase,
my heart is nearly deceased,

I think of you and all you could be doing,
The more I ponder, the worse the pain ensuing.

These heart pangs are from you,
but even if that's true,

No matter what you do,
I'll always want you.

I LOST IT

It's been misplaced,
my precious heart cannot be replaced,

And yet, I lost possession.
What a position...

Did I give it away and forget to get it back?
I've clumsily fallen for many people, my heart
stained black.

From all the times it had been dropped,
it is mine to fix...

After a while, sentiment turns into resentment,
Many messages were typed that were never sent.

I don't know how to properly vent,
You're a derelict tenant who never pays rent,

I can't keep up with forgetting you,
I can't go one day without thinking about you,
In the following days, you will haunt me, too.

PURGATORY

I can't get away from you,
I wonder if you are stuck too.
You dwell in the heart of my mind,
And so my soul is truly in a bind.

I dwell on the verge of sanity,
Finding solace in insanity.
This is true torture,
Looking forward to the future,
But held back by the past.
How long will my pain last?

I see you every day but am never truly with you
Is this what love is supposed to do?
If so, I hate it with every fiber of my being,
Unable to move on, no matter how hard I've been
seeking.

I want to love and reap love,
Yet I can't replace your love.
Even when you aren't here,
Your voice lingers in my ear,
Beckoning me to stay and wait for you.

That's selfish, even if I desire to someday.
It's not like I didn't wait…
I waited for your love to recuperate,
To find what we had, even if it had been lost.

My heart yearns,
My heart burns,
Clinging to the fallacy of a happy ending
between us,
Knowing well it can never be the same
between us.

I'll fight, and then I'll stay,
Hoping you'd come back to me, someday
This may be the end of our story,
Until I know, I'm trapped in purgatory.

PILLS

What should I take for heartache?
My heart continues to shake.
What prescription
Will null my affliction?

What kind of tissues
Can dry the tears caused by my heart's issues?
Can I ever recover from this pain,
With every memory haunting my brain?

They linger in my heart,
Impeding recovery before it can start.

Symptoms include:
Solitude,
Nausea,
Insomnia,
Heartaches,
Heartbreaks,
Stress,

Societal mess,
Teary eyes,
Loud cries,
And other variations.

What creations,
What unstable trick,
Could possibly fix
This broken heart?

Emotional connections now fail to spark,
My heart lies dormant in the dark.

It will hurt until I find the remedy—
To fight my heartache and society,
Or fall to the numbing effects of thrills,
Succumbing to the consumption of pills.

ONE NIGHT

The only thing on my mind tonight is how much I
want to unwind,
Have a long conversation with no other intention.

We talked as I expected,
But the conversation consumed me—my plate
was neglected.

After a while of laughs, I silently hoped the night
would last.
I had high hopes coming in, thinking our time
was just beginning.

You asked if we could go to my place,
And I couldn't resist the grin on your face.
I took your hand, and we went,

By the time we reached the bedroom, I was hellbent.
Being desired by you—was better than sex,
Pulling me into the possibility of what could come
next.

I had to stop to catch my breath before I got
further,
Doing my best to hold my composure.

Damp hands betrayed the excitement I tried to
hide,
A fight to tame the butterflies swarming inside.

What would happen if we gave in too soon?
Would the passion fade with the moon?

Judgments clouded, emotions twisted,
Is this real? Does she feel what I feel?

But still, I let you have your way,
Hoping beyond hope that you would stay.

So I said, "If you want me tonight, tomorrow, or anytime,
I'll be there at the drop of a dime."

I gave in to you as you gave in to me,
Your moans a symphonic harmony.

As the night concluded, so did we,
Leaving nothing but regret and misery.

Morning came, and I woke up alone.

DON'T SMILE

At the highest peak where I stand, one foot off,
looking down at the land.
I ponder one thing before I rue, You.

I was struck by your smile, why was I affected by
your smile!?

Maybe solitude weakened my guard for you;
maybe your smile, I simply wasn't used to.

Your dazzling special smile! Brought back a feeling
I hadn't felt in a while.

When you smiled for me to see, something
changed, inside of me.

Your smile found its way to my broken part and
shined a light on a black and beaten heart.

Why? Did your smile make me believe I had
to try?
I removed the only stable foot I had to keep me
sane,
Disregarded every warning from my brain.
I CLOSED MY EYES AND FELL,
For you.
My eyes slowly started to swell,
BECAUSE I KNEW, DAMN WELL.

You would never catch me...
So here I enter, the state of free fall, wondering
why I did it all,

For your smile.
I wanted to believe my life would shift,
That you had other reasons for showing me such
a precious gift.

But here I am, falling to my fate, before the privilege of a first date.
Even when I recover and am told there will be another,

I shudder...
At the thought of falling again, and again.
So next time, just know for my sake,
That for every time my heart breaks.

I must climb higher and higher,
You were my desire, but now I tire.

I shall finish my fall, climb back to safety,
Wishing you had never noticed me.

For me, it's not worthwhile,
So please, don't smile.

DON'T FALL FOR ME

I stand, a broken refrain,
a heart too wounded to love again,

You approach with warmth, your love is aglow,
but my heart, in darkness, refuses to grow.

"Why? Why the distance?" Your eyes implore,
yet my silence speaks of pain galore,

I'm not blind to your love, I can see,
but in the storm, I choose to be, pain-free.

Keep walking, just let me be,
for love's tender call, I cannot decree,

I fear the future, where love may fade,
in this fragile heart, where scars are made.

Your affection, a beacon, in the night,
but my soul's trapped in a never-ending fight,

I've tasted love's bitterness, felt its sting,
a fragile heart, I cannot bring.

You may like me now but may not love me later,
I can't lift another finger, I can't bear the shame,

You wish to save me, to light my way,
but these waters, I've learned to sway.

I won't let you fall in love's deep blue,
for I know, my dear, I won't catch you,

It's not that I'm cold or devoid of care,
but my heart's too heavy, my burden to bear.

So, walk away from this weary soul,
to another, let your love find its goal,

For in your absence, I find my peace,
a broken heart, with pain to cease.

HEART IN AN UBER

No idea if our expectations would be met.
Before the night, I imagined how it might go—
Moonlit walks, a slow, steady flow.

My hands shook as I tied my tie to an acceptable
knot, Hoping she'd accept me, as I am or am not.

Heart pounding when her ringtone chimed—
A text: "I'm waiting, mister."
I checked my reflection, nerves rising,
Gripped the wheel, knuckles white, trying not to
be late.

When I saw her, my heart raced—
Magnificent in every way, her smile lit up her face.
We walked through a park, moonlight guiding our
steps.

On the bridge, I whispered, "This is the best date
I've ever had,"

Kissed her cheek, her hand warm in mine.
She smiled and said, "Take me back to your place."

I paused, but with her, time felt irrelevant.
Back at my apartment, something shifted,
Her gaze was bold, her touch insistent.

Suddenly, she was leading the night—
Her desire ignited a fire in me.
Before I could grasp it, we were lost in each other,
My mind struggling to keep pace with my body.

By the time we finished, she rolled over, satisfied,
While I lay there, trying to make sense of the
speed, intensity, and the shift in tone.

I held her, imagining a future lifting off my chest,
Thinking the night would become something
more.

I fell asleep with hope,
But woke to emptiness.

Alone in bed,

A note on her pillow read:
"Thanks for last night, I called an Uber."

TARNISHED

Once I beheld you, a pristine tome, a bound
beauty, a sanctuary, a cherished home,

Afraid to touch, your cover untouched, I admired
from afar, my desires hushed.

Yet in the whispers, I heard the tale, of hands that
wandered without fail,

Your package torn, your cover bruised, access
granted, desire profused.

I hesitated, my interest waned, as more hands
upon you, freely gained,

No judgment passed, no scorn, just rue, for the
allure of mystery was now askew.

You were the book I longed to read, but now a
story with a tainted creed,

If I dared to flip your pages, worn, would I forget
how you were once adorned?

Your spine, once straight, now gently bent, a
narrative of consents, freely lent,

Yet shallow, it feels, this waning desire,
as I yearn for love, purer, entire.

To read you now with tainted eyes,
would I see the truth amidst the lies?

Could I forget the hands that traced
the contours of your pages, embraced?

You, a book once cherished, pristine and fair,
now a story told, of love laid bare,

In the margins, the history etched,
a consensual tale, yet love's perfection, fetched.

Shall I brave the chapters, explore your lore,
or let you rest, as memories implore?

For you, a book, once new and bright,
are now a tale of consensual delight.

BREAK UP CLASS

Let's do the math, and unravel this equation; we
once shared love, now just a vague sensation,

Like numbers on a board, we added and
subtracted, but our love story got somehow
redacted.

You can't change angles, geometry's rule, our
paths diverged, it's no longer cool,

Like parallel lines, we never did meet,
in the realm of love, our story's now fleet.

You used to run through my mind, swift as a
track, but now you're just a shadow, nothing I
lack,

Our relationship faded, like ink on paper,
no chemistry left, just the lingering vapor.

I speak the language of love, fluent in emotion,
your words are mere echoes, lost in the ocean,

I don't understand the phrases you weave,
our history is history, it's time we both leave.

WHEN HE SPEAKS

When he speaks,
He knocks prominently on my chest,
Growing more persistent when I try to ignore him.

When he speaks,
He articulates words that cut through everything,
Knowing just what to say and how to say it.
A tear comes to my eye,
Because my feelings match his words.

When he speaks,
I feel relief,
A peace breaking through my gray depressive
state.
Because when he speaks, he tells the raw,
undeniable truth.

When he speaks,
I listen, because he won't relent otherwise.
His persistence is too powerful to delay.
He told me to write it all down and read it until I
could find happiness.

When he spoke,
He helped me face the reality I was hiding.

He said,
"We are broken, that's a fact.
We hide from pain, afraid to love again.
But it's time to pick up the pieces,
Because the pain of loving hurts less than the
pain of silence."

He was tired of waiting in silence,
Tired of hurting, and he knew I was too.
"We need to love again, without regret.
Lost love is a choice—don't make it."
And in that moment, my heart and I had a
breakthrough.

It's time to follow his lead,
To love with confidence,

Because, rarely, I am so moved when he speaks.

THE GAMES WE PLAY

I don't care how you feel.
I do care how you feel.
When I slide myself inside,
I don't care what's inside

I just want to get off,
So I need you to get on.
What did you expect? This ain't a love song.
I'm not here for long.

You'll cry alone, blame me to your friends,
Say I'm the reason trust in men always ends.
You'll sob in your bed, clutching your phone,
But I promise, you'll never hear my ringtone.

What I care about is simple:
I want to win,
To play with your heart,
And plant doubt within.

You're oblivious to it all,
So I set the perfect trap, knowing you'd fall.
Hey, It's okay, I fell for it too,
Dust yourself off; now it's on you.

I, like them, am not here to commit.
I'll win our game, I'll make you submit.
This game is cruel, I dont give a shit.
Once you get played, you'll learn to play it.

I know the rules, perfected the technique,
To conquer you, a task not unique.

Hurt people, hurt people, it's where I excel.
In this cruel game, I play them too well.

Sometimes I wonder when I'm through,
If the losers I've played, Will play the game too.

STATION 4

Poems of Depression, Regret & Mourning

"Yeah, you thought station 3 was a bit rough? This is where my hopelessness, remorse, fear, frustration, & negative self-talk reside. To be completely transparent, it's an ugly place to be, but it happens. I had to process it, and seeing it helped me get through it."

TAINTED

I tried once to clean
to wash mind of memory
of us, you and I.

TRAPPED

I'm trapped in my mind, *Am I going crazy?*
Hoping that you'd love me, please don't call me
"lazy,"
I built these damn walls, but my memories are
hazy.

I'm trapped in my mind, *What do they want
from me?*
They fear me, I know,
yet I am locked without a key.

I built this cage and imagined they'd hate me.
Deep inside, my resentment burned like Hades.

I'm trapped in my mind, *Am I afraid to leave?*
I don't know what I need, just thought I needed reprieve.

I'm trapped in my mind, stoicism my facade,
I hide myself away, though I crave to be odd.

I'm trapped in my mind, *I think I'm getting closer,*
To finding myself and reassembling my composure.

I'm trapped in my mind, *I know what this is about.*
But now it feels like, I'm never getting out.

I'm trapped in my mind...

DENIAL

After a while, the clock turns a dial,

And my life is shortened, as I sit and try to
comprehend,

Where this time is going—what have I learned?
How am I growing?

Confusion brews, frustration ensues,
Time keeps ticking, I know it's wasting,
So why does my heart keep racing?

I can't stop searching.
For a moment to live for, sitting is simple
but I'm going mental.

Why am I stuck?
Time keeps ticking, I'm out of luck.

The joys and sorrows of the past, masked by my fallacies,
Of a better tomorrow, removed from sorrow—
A tale written for fantasies.

But the feeling I get when my mind tries to pick,
As the time continues to tick,

I'm lost inside myself—this can't be good for my health.

Yet I remain dormant, enduring the torment.

My mind feels like it's on trial,
As I sit here, trapped in denial.

POSSESSED

What phenomena,
Living through relationship trauma,

PTSD is a scar in my mind,
My memorial flashbacks are buried deep in my
subconscious in the hopes they are harder to find,

Echoes of laughter, shadows of touch, in the
depths of my soul, they clutch,

A sound, a scent, a reminiscent gleam, brings you
back like a recurring dream.

In my mind's eye, and although I thought I could
no longer cry,

When I am caught off guard by your presence, it
makes me reminisce,

And in the end, I just pretend,
That without you I can be found, somewhere deep
within myself I am certainly bound,

Possessed by memories, I struggle to sever,
Chained to the past, haunted forever.

DISAPPEAR

I am in fear of what I hear,
When I'm alone to think. Deep inside where I
reside, my thoughts cause me to sink.

Sadness, a vast, uncharted sea, threatens to
consume the core of me.

I try to navigate away from the madness but steer
into a torrent of sadness.

I yearn to escape, to find my way, for madness
looms where my thoughts stay.

Yet, within sanity, there's no sanctuary found,
only echoes of love now underground.

I cannot bear to ponder, to reminisce, to hold
your ghost in a lover's kiss.

Avoiding the truth, my refuge and my rue,
I deny what once was me and you.

Afraid of what lies beyond the veer,
in denial, I make my escape clear.

I disappear into shadows and fear,
refusing the truth until I reappear.

Only to vanish once again,
as if this cycle has no end.

BEFORE THE FALL

Before the fall,
My senses awaken, a prelude to the storm,
A symphony of emotions, starting to form.

My ears catch the whispers of sorrow's song,
A melody of melancholy, promising tomorrow
won't belong.

My nose detects the scent of impending rain,
the petrichor of tears, a harbinger of pain,

My eyes shimmer, caught in the watery dance,
Reflecting the depth of this internal trance.

My cheeks feel the weight of the storm's pour,
Tickled by teardrops I can't ignore.

My senses tell a tale untold,
Of a heart heavy, of emotions bold.

In this prelude, a storm brews within,
Feelings rise, ready to begin.

Before the fall, in my senses, I confide—
The urge to cry, was impossible to hide.

TIME

In the echo of my hurried words, I said I had no
time for you,
But deep down, I knew that wasn't true.

"I can't make time," I said, trying to hide,
But really, it was fear that I let slide.

Excuses wrapped in moments too few,
Yet time bends for what we choose to pursue.

"I don't have time for this," I said, feeling strained,
Avoiding the places where my fears reigned.

Like sand through my fingers, moments slipped
away,
But in every grain, there was so much to say.

"I can't make time for you," a lie I told out of fear,
Hoping you wouldn't notice as I disappeared.

Time, the architect of what we build, plays its part,
But my anxiety kept me from the start.

"I don't have time," I said, avoiding the crowd,
Afraid of what they'd think, afraid to be loud.

In the weave of moments, where life entwines,
I let go of the threads that held us in line.
"I can't make time," an excuse I tried to live by,
But love always knows when my truth lies.

So here I stand, in the shards of what we were,
Longing for the time that once was hers.

"I don't have time," now haunts me still,
For in your absence, time's void is all I feel.

WAIT FOR ME

Words cannot explain how you departed me,
The last breath that left your lungs,
The last rhythmic beat of your delicate heart,

Started a flood that ran down my cheeks until my
sheets were drenched and my ducts were dry.

I cried for more than who you were but also who
you didn't become.
Overcome by visualizations of your endless
potential and possibilities.
Tossed aside by the end of all things.

Occasionally, dear friend, I consciously conjured constructive plans to join you.
But I was thwarted by the look I saw on your face...

When you saw me again for the first time, it seemed all too similar.
The same face that I wear on my face now.

So, I concluded that nothing I could do would be worse than seeing your heavenly tears,
And so, I ask you to please wait for what will eventually be,
Please, my dear friend, "wait for me."

TODAY

I laid down a little too long today,
I had plans to go, but I had to stay.

I stared out the window too long today,
Escaping the world in my own quiet way.

I listened to my music play too long today,
Tunes were washing waves keeping my worries
at bay.

I thought about my life too long today,
How it all seemed to weigh on me, in every way.

So I laid down a little too long today,
Let my bed hold me close in its soft sway.

Because when nothing really seems to go my way,
I use days like today, to cry my worries away.

The sun shines too bright for me today,
I surrender to the darkness, come what may.

I laid down a little too long today,
For days like this, I think it's quite okay.

DEPRESSION

Oh, Depression, the diagnosis of this session.
As I lay on the elongated chair,
I watch my counselor as I scratch my hair.

"Depression, you say?"
"Yes," she replies, "but let me help, if I may."
"We can fix this."
I weirdly felt a sense of relief, though it wasn't the
happiness I missed.

I assumed I was so accustomed to the depression
That it seemed to me like a normal expression.
Honestly, I feel as though it helps me appreciate
the little pleasures—
All those memorable treasures.

"Fixing means something must be broken," I retort.
"I don't feel broken, but take my words as a token
Of my gratitude for your care and concern.
But I don't yearn.
To be forever happy."
"That may be denial or lunacy." she quips.
Maybe I am delusional, but I have never had the luxury
Of even dreaming of a life full of happiness and positivity.

"Why is that not something to shoot for?" she asks.
"Don't you want more than your pessimistic outlook on things?"
"Don't confuse me for a pessimist, dear counselor;
A realist, indeed, though I often dwell in my dreams.

Regardless, I must thank you again for your
sympathy."
"I've been there before...it is empathy," she says.

"Though sadly, we will have to conclude this
session."
"Come back next week to continue our
discussion."

"All right, I guess we can figure this out,
and release some tension.
But don't worry about me—it's just Depression."

I CAN SMILE

I can smile.
I can make your time worthwhile.
I hope you do not mind if my face is often idle.
I am fighting suicidal.

I can smile.
All the while. All my worries seem to pile.
Both my eyes flow like the Nile.
Although, I still know how to smile.

I can smile.
I need a number, I can dial. I found a vial.
I lie down for a while. I spew out bile. I feel my
blood spread along the tile.
I do my best to hold on to my smile.
In denial. In a while. In space filled with sorrow.
In freedoms presence from tomorrow.
In my heart, I felt so hollow.
In my throat, the pain was hard to swallow.

I can smi...

WHO SHOT YA?

Final breaths taste sweeter, a bitter encore,
Life hangs by a thread, as it has for those before.

In this moment, shadows dance on the wall,
A waltz in red and blue, as sirens softly call.

I'm fixated on the hand that quivers,
Fingers wet, like rain on shivering rivers.

I stand with fate, eye to eye,
My life in your hands, under this darkened sky.

Time ticks like a bomb, each second a drumbeat,
Heartbeats echo, like distant, thunderous feet.

Fear coils around my throat like a tightening
noose;
In the silence, gunmetal glints, a lethal pose.

The air's electric, charged with primal fear,
Generations' weight, all carried here.

I see my ancestors in this midnight's hush—
Their silent screams, their hearts crushed.

Eyes lock, a battle of wills that's never fair.
I stand here, knowing history stares.

The past echoes, in the cold, still air,
Futures cut short, lives lost in despair.

Final breaths taste sweeter as adrenaline roars,
Life's tapestry unraveled on the cold, unforgiving
floors.

In this moment, where time seems to suspend,
I pray for mercy, my life is on a precipice, about
to end.

VILLAIN

My delinquency did not originate within me,
The path was set for horrific tribulations,
Brought about by recurring sensations.

Situationally stable, yet I am set,
To commit atrocities—
Whose civic duty lies in embodying the hero who
saves the cities?

Who are those who designate me
To be your enemy?

Haunted paths, created by those before me,
I did not fail; I simply adapted for survivability.

Conscience will always bear down upon me,
In the shadows of my nightmares,
The midnight scares.
Tread softly with my fears,

Because fear is my reality,
Tortured by the paths paved intentionally.

I found the best outcomes from the worst
situations,
With similar variations.

I stood tall every moment that I could,
Before being knocked down and bashed by
"would."

"Would I," "Could I," and "Should I"—
These led to many things I regret.
The cost of opportunity, I must never forget.

A powerful victim, a slave to my desire,
My urges and whims, an unquenchable fire.

Do I terrorize your social norms?
With my outrageous uproars that take numerous
forms?

The only reason you see me in this light
Is because you didn't walk in my shoes in the
night.

I dwell in the night where my story lies within.
In your story, I am the villain.

STATION 5

*Poems of Gratitude,
Nostalgia, Appreciation*

*"Congratulations! You made it out of
the dark into the light of gratitude and
appreciation. This is the last chapter
that I have to offer. I deeply appreciate
that you made it this far, dear reader. I
tried to write as raw and authentically as
possible because that's my truest form.
Hopefully, you found a few relatable
poems to take with you after you are
done. See you at the end of the line."*

LOVE

Submit to the pain
To truly feel the depth of
love that is and was

FORGETTING
TO FORGET

What kind of storms can cloud the memories of
reading to each other aloud?

What kind of thunder can smother the sounds of
your soft snore in slumber?

What force can dim my thoughts of you, of
dreams we dared and plans we drew?

In pain, your memory is steadfast and clear,
in the core of my soul, you remain near.

There lies a sanctum, both resilient and bright,
where storms cease, in pure, serene light.

Recollections of us may bring tears, yet I smile at the love that erased fears.

We've bid farewell, yet echoes remain, in the chambers of my heart, your love's refrain.

As new tales unfold, and I move ahead, I'll cherish what was where our love once tread.

I'll hold to memories, both joyous and bittersweet, embracing the love that made my heartbeat.

In my heart, your love remains an eternal silhouette.

I will never regret, forgetting to forget.

WORTH IT

Late-night rants about who wears the pants,

Midnight memories height, saying good night,

Watching the hours fly on the phone, ruing the
dial tone,

Even as it grew late, together we were great,

Mine was yours and yours was mine, we always
shared the time,

Even if we fought, our ties were taut,
I felt I never deserved it, but loving you was
worth it.

STAR GIRL

I've never played with a star before,
And therefore, the opportunity meant more.

Then I could even fathom,
When we were together at night,
you shined so bright.

Your smile seemed to sparkle.
Starlight, you shine so damn bright,

That's how I know, how much I need you,
You light my sky dear, when darkness spreads fear.

While you were singing,
The Weeknd on a weekend,
My walls began to weaken.

I appreciated our time together,
Every moment, every night you pointed out the
Big Dipper.
It's not the constellation I long to see,
The star that means most is much closer to me.

You helped me enjoy the night skies,
Now, I'm stargazing you with a new set of eyes,
And I need you to realize,
You're my Star Girl

FREEDOM

Enormous walls with palisade,
I lay dormant in a prison that was self-made.

A tempest roared, lashed at my tower,
True care's tears fell like a gentle shower.

"Believe in yourself," thundered a lover dear,
Sincerity echoing, dispelling fear.

Your storm, a marvelous view,
Through Thunder's voice, I grasped the cue.

I rose, my barriers began to crumble,
embraced the world, no longer humble.

Gratitude blooms for your tempest's grace,
in newfound freedom, I find my place.

NOT SO SIMPLE MAN

You were goofy, you were kind,
You meant a lot to me, how your smile would
shine.

You made me want to be better, smarter,
healthier, gentler, and kinder.

You were not a simple man; the way you
motivated me, I could not fully understand.

You crafted dreams with hands of gold,
In your wisdom, my story was told.

A mentor, not just in name, your legacy, a burning
flame.

I hope I can be what you were to somebody,

Because who's better than you?
Nobody.

MOON

Our Daddy loved to party,
So much so that he made multiple nightclubs,
and successful nights fed his little cubs.

He'd tell stories of how his music was crunk,
His breath was strongly laced with liquor, the
common signs he was drunk,

He could handle it, we cubs learned to embrace it.

Daddy came back to the house, loud and naughty,
But at the end of the day, he still loved to party.

We young cubs grew up to be big bears, and the
first thing on our minds was the effect of beers,

And all the other liquors that we could consume,
growing up watching our father we presumed.

That there was no other, pleasure, than being out
with the moon,

So, we played in the nighttime moonlight, and
soon,
We found out just why our Daddy loved the
moon.

ODE TO DAD

This for the best mentor I know,

My fearsome father, always prepared to lend me a
hand,
No matter how hard I fall, he would help me stand,

As one of my number-one fans,
You would not miss an event or a moment to
enhance,

My growth as a man, I hope you understand,

How you affected me, how much of an
impression you left on me,

I am who you brought me up to be,
I am not perfect, neither are you,
But I like who I am,

Although there are some moments when I wish I
were more like you,

In the end, you were a great dad.

ODE TO MAMA

This is for the strongest woman I know,
You taught me much and loved me so,

My mighty mama, you taught me so many things
indirectly,
Like how to love correctly,

You loved me through your work ethic,
Making sure, I was provided for,

You loved me through your smile,
That made me feel like I was worthwhile,

You loved me through your trust in me,
Although sometimes I rebelled,
I could tell that you knew I'd do the right thing,

And even if I didn't...that I learned from it,

You loved me – that's all I need to keep on going,

Knowing I have such a great momma, who adores me.

Thank you so much, momma.

IRREPLACEABLE

Motivated by the late great Nat King Cole,
Who spoke of a muse that was unforgettable,

I came to the realization that throughout my life,
I have been replaceable, that premise was
inescapable.

With my classmates and friends, the trend never
ends,

I have been erased from their memory,
Or smashed into a fragment of what I used to be.

To put it simply, I am replaceable, in every sense
of the word,

My lovers have moved on to their seconds or thirds,

The only people to keep me close are those who
love me the most.

My family has been, and will always be, reliable,
I know that to them, I am irreplaceable.

UGLY BOY

Daunted by the mirror's reflection,
Self-love was my only protection.

Even with the love in me, I cannot best society,

True beauty lies in the ratio,
a golden face, attractive beau.

Self-love is a daily battle,
Sex sells, it feeds the cattle.

Attraction, a primal feel,
Love means naught, as the third wheel…

Love is often outshined by the shallow expectations
of the blind.

They do not understand, for me, it's hard to be suave,
First impressions mean everything, yet I do not improv.

I know what you see, I spend countless hours trying
to improve,
Chasing affection, hoping you would approve.

They say, "You can do better," and I agree.
You know they're wrong, they cannot see.
The inside that holds my identity.

You don't care how I look but how I cradle your heart,
How I make you laugh and smile and call you
"sweetheart."

How I make you dinner and giggle and take you on
dates.

How I only see you, and I know I won first place.

To the victor goes the spoils, so I'll spoil you often,
Just love me, don't leave me, I promise, I'll soften.

No mirrors glare, no judgments cold, can tarnish the
love that we hold.

For in your love, I am set free, embracing all that's
truly me.

GOOD ENOUGH

Friendship is rare and it's hard to perceive,
with you all, I truly believe.

You know me, you like what you see,
with you around, I feel like somebody.

True friends are there through and through,
they see your soul, and they speak to you.

Amidst the masks, you cherish what's real,
in your presence, my authentic self I reveal.

Genuine bonds, unspoken and true,
nurtured from seeds, to trees they grew.

Laughter echoes, tears we share,
And strength in unity, beyond compare.

Through thick and thin, your support remains,
in trials and tribulations, you soothe my pains.

A tapestry woven with threads of gold,
with friends like you, my heart unfolds.

No judgment here, henceforth,
a sanctuary found on this vast earth.

We laugh, we cry, we strengthen our tether,
birds of a feather, flock together.

I'm grateful for you, a priceless find,
in the vast universe, you're one of a kind.

With friends like you, I'm strong and tough,
in your embrace, I am good enough.

DEAR DAD

Dear Dad,
I never had my breath stolen from me
Until you breathed your last.
On May 19th, I prayed for a chance to save you.
I'm so sorry, there was nothing I could do.

Dear Dad,
I woke up and realized it was the first day,
On the first day, I had to spend a full day
In this world without you.
I don't want to be in a world without you,
But sadly, I have to.

Dear Dad,
It hurts so much to love you now.
It hurts to know that the smile I love, the laugh I
love, and the guidance I yearned for
Will be no more.

Dear Dad,
How do I even begin to cook as well as you did?
How could I find the amount of love you poured
into every dish?
Dad, I wish

I could take all the love you poured into me, and
use every ounce to be the person you wanted me
to be.

I know I was on the right path,
Because while you were with me, you said as
much.

"I love you and I'm proud of you" will forever
reside within me.

I'm proud of you too, Dad.

Dear Dad,
It hurts every day to love you so much.
We had thousands of hugs, yet I miss your touch.
I don't want the pain to go away.
I want to remember you clearly,
Through open ears, a prideful heart, and your
presence, your love you did convey.
Father, yesterday, today, and tomorrow, I'll miss
you dearly.

Dear Dad,
I'll hold you close to my heart
If pain is what it costs while we are apart,
I'll pay it every day beyond death do us part.

-Love your son, Parker

"Emotions are a mosaic of our human experience. Every feeling of joy, sorrow, love, regret ~ has a beauty all its own. Sometimes, the hardest feelings that we bear can shape us the most, giving our lives more depth and color. If there's one truth these poems have taught me, it's that each emotion has a purpose, and even the darkest moments hold potential for growth if they are harnessed. May these words remind you of the strength and beauty in **every** feeling that resides within you."

THE END

About the Author

Parker Tillman is a poet whose work explores love, loss, identity, and the nuances of personal growth. Born and raised in Grand Rapids, Michigan, he values family, integrity, and self-reflection. His journey with poetry began in high school but truly took root at Northwood University, where he won a poetry competition for his piece When I Lost You (KISS).

After a five-year hiatus, Parker returned to his craft, completing Stations Along My Train of Thought, a collection reflecting on his turbulent college years. Through his words, he invites readers to join him on a journey of self-discovery and reflection. Beyond poetry, Parker is an athlete, real estate investor, and hopes to write children's books on financial literacy and ethics, helping young readers understand important concepts early in life.

"Throughout my life, writing has been my compass— helping me navigate the highs and lows, the victories and losses. It became a way to communicate with myself, a release for what I couldn't express vocally. Expression, I've come to learn, isn't about perfection; it's about honesty. For some, it might come in words; for others, it might be through music, art, movement, or even silence.

My hope is that as you close these pages, you'll carry with you the sense that every emotion you feel deserves a place. Whatever form it takes, find a way to let it out and make it your own. Expression is one of life's most beautiful acts—giving voice to what's within and honoring who you truly are."

Now Disembarking: The Train of Thought